Author:
John Malam studied ancient history and archeology at the University of Birmingham, England, after which he worked as an archeologist at the Ironbridge Gorge Museum in Shropshire, England. He is now an author, specializing in nonfiction books for children. He lives in Cheshire, England, with his wife and their two children. Find out more at: www.johnmalam.co.uk

Artist:
David Antram was born in Brighton, England, in 1958. He studied at Eastbourne College of Art and then worked in advertising for fifteen years before becoming a full-time artist. He has illustrated many children's nonfiction books.

Series creator:
David Salariya was born in Dundee, Scotland. He has illustrated a wide range of books and has created and designed many new series for publishers in the UK and overseas. He established The Salariya Book Company in 1989. He lives in Brighton, England, with his wife, illustrator Shirley Willis, and their son, Jonathan.

Editor: **Tanya Kant**

Editorial Assistant: **Mark Williams**

© The Salariya Book Company Ltd MMIX

No part of this publication may be reproduced in whole or in part, or stored in a retrieval system, or transmitted in any form or by any means, electronic, mechanical, photocopying, recording, or otherwise, without written permission of the publisher. For information regarding permission, write to the copyright holder.

Published in Great Britain in 2009 by
The Salariya Book Company Ltd
25 Marlborough Place, Brighton BN1 1UB

ISBN-13: 978-0-531-20824-3 (lib. bdg.) 978-0-531-21048-2 (pbk.)
ISBN-10: 0-531-20824-9 (lib. bdg.) 0-531-21048-0 (pbk.)

All rights reserved.
Published in 2009 in the United States
by Franklin Watts
An imprint of Scholastic Inc.
Published simultaneously in Canada.

A CIP catalog record for this book is available
from the Library of Congress.

Printed and bound in China.
Printed on paper from sustainable sources.

SCHOLASTIC, FRANKLIN WATTS, and associated logos are trademarks and/or registered trademarks of Scholastic Inc.

You Wouldn't Want to Be a Skyscraper Builder!

DRRRR!

Written by
John Malam

Illustrated by
David Antram

Created and designed by
David Salariya

A Hazardous Job You'd Rather Not Take

Franklin Watts®
An Imprint of Scholastic Inc.
NEW YORK • TORONTO • LONDON • AUCKLAND • SYDNEY
MEXICO CITY • NEW DELHI • HONG KONG
DANBURY, CONNECTICUT

Contents

Introduction

How much worse can it get? Like millions of other workers in the United States during the Great Depression, you're out of a job. Every day you walk the streets of New York City, looking for work. You've been doing this for months, but no matter where you go, the message is always the same: No work.

It hasn't always been this hard. Until last year, you had a job as a builder and had enough money to buy food and pay the bills. But then came October 29, 1929—Black Tuesday. It was a day of panic in the business world, and within hours companies had lost millions of dollars. Unable to pay workers' wages, these companies had to lay off many people. It was the start of the Great Depression—a time of poverty and hardship.

You lost your job, but that doesn't mean you've given up hope! You've heard about a project to build a huge new skyscraper in Manhattan, one of the wealthiest parts of New York City. Stay positive, and maybe you'll find work there.

NO WORK

Will I ever get a job?

5

Sky High!

Speech bubbles in illustration:
- Tasty apples. Only five cents.
- Five cents?! I'm not made of money!

New York City Rises

The island of Manhattan is the heart of New York City. It's packed with shops, hotels, and offices, and has become so crowded that new buildings have to grow up rather than out. It's no wonder that New York is famous for its skyscrapers. By the end of the 1920s, there are 15 towers more than 500 feet (152 m) high. But while the city is growing, your life has fallen apart. You've been out of work since Black Tuesday, and you're one of about 6,000 unemployed people scraping together a living on the streets of New York.

Boom and Bust

BOOM. Before the Depression, there was plenty of work for everyone. When one building job was finished, you moved on to the next. Life was good.

Speech bubble: I'm broke!

1929: BLACK TUESDAY. Fortunes were lost when the stock market suddenly collapsed.

BUST. The firm you worked for went out of business. You are now one of millions out of work.

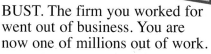

1913: Woolworth Building. 60 stories, 792 feet (241 m)

1908: Singer Building. 47 stories, 613 feet (187 m)

1909: Metropolitan Life Insurance Tower. 50 stories, 700 feet (213 m)

1894: Manhattan Life Insurance Building. 17 stories, 348 feet (106 m)

Handy Hint

Ask around. Other men might know where there's work to be found.

1846: Trinity Church. 281 feet (86 m)

1875: New York Tribune Building. 9 stories, 260 feet (79 m)

1902: Flatiron Building. 22 stories, 285 feet (87 m)

1890: New York World Building. 18 stories, 309 feet (94 m)

1889: Tower Building. 11 stories, 160 feet (49 m)

Note: Buildings are not shown in their actual locations.

Wrecker! It's Your Job

After selling apples on the street for a few weeks, your luck has changed. You've gotten a job as a wrecker on a demolition site. It's dangerous work, but the pay is good: a dollar an hour. The site is at the corner of 5th Avenue and 34th Street, where more than 600 workers are demolishing the Waldorf-Astoria Hotel to make room for a new skyscraper. By February 1930, your job is done. About 15,000 tons of iron and steel are hauled away to be recycled, and thousands of tons of rubble are dumped at sea.

Going, going, gone!

HIGH-CLASS HOTEL. Opened in 1897, the Waldorf-Astoria was New York's grandest hotel. It had more than 1,000 rooms.

AUCTION SALE. When the hotel closed, the contents were sold.

FIREWOOD. Scrap wood from the demolition of the hotel is left for the poor to take.

This is high-class firewood!

Dangers of Demolition

Blinding sparks

Sharp splinters and rusty nails

Falling debris

Thunk!

Deadly falls

Bad cuts

8

It's a Blast!

STEP BY STEP. Sticks of dynamite are put in holes drilled in the rock. Wires join the explosives. Iron covers laid over the holes stop debris from flying out.

1. Drilling

2. Charging

3. Wiring

4. Covering

Kaboom! Blasters at Work

With the old hotel out of the way, it's time to dig the foundation pit for the new skyscraper. You join a team of blasters whose job is to use explosives to clear away loose soil and rock.

The quickest way to clear the loose soil and rock is to blow them up. You operate a bone-shaking drill. It's so loud that it damages your hearing.* This could be a problem—if you can't hear the warning whistle, you might get caught in the blast! But you need the work so you keep drilling holes for the next ground-splitting explosion. As you blast your way across the site, earth-moving machines follow you, moving the rubble away.

* Ear protection has been invented, but most workers at this time don't like to wear it.

NOISES. A whistle is the signal to take cover. You hear a dull thud from the ground, and the iron covers are forced up by the explosion.

5. Warning

Danger Zone!

FATAL ACCIDENT. One man is killed when he runs into the blast area and is caught in the explosion.

6. THUD!

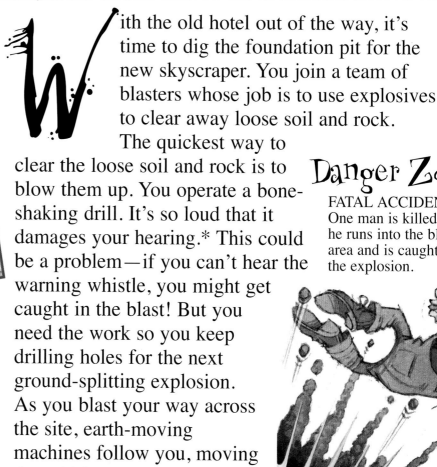

Rock Bottom! Deep Hole

The skyscraper will be called the Empire State Building,* and it must be ready by May 1931. In less than 18 months, the world's tallest building will stand where you are now! On days when there's no blasting in the foundation pit, you work as a ground man, guiding the huge bucket of a steam shovel as it clears rubble. Be careful: don't get crushed by falling rocks! After digging deep and clearing away all the debris, you find what you want—solid bedrock. Now that you've hit "rock bottom," it's time to start raising the tower.

"Empire State" is a nickname for New York State.

Get out of the way!

Night and Day

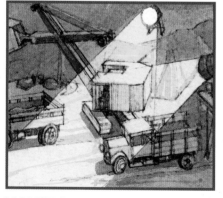

NONSTOP. The foundation pit is dug 39 feet (12 m) into the ground. Work goes on through the night.

SHOVELS. Four steam shovels scoop up the loose rock. Each shovel has three men to work it.

CRANES. Three steam-powered cranes haul the material and equipment into and out of the pit.

DERRICKS. Stiff-leg derricks reach places cranes can't. Three of them are on-site.

TRUCKS. By March 1930, 28,529 truckloads of debris have been carried away from the site.

13

Bare Bones! A Steel Skeleton

Help! I'm stuck in the sticky stuff!

Grab my hand!

I t's Monday, March 17, 1930, and the first pieces of the skyscraper's steel skeleton are brought in from Pittsburgh, 388 miles (624 km) from New York City. The furnaces of America's greatest steel city have been burning around the clock to make the steel beams in time. When they arrive, the beams are still warm! Each beam is numbered and lowered into the correct hole that's been drilled down to bedrock. Tons of concrete have been poured into the holes, and as the concrete hardens, the beams are locked into the bedrock. Be careful—with metal, holes, and concrete everywhere, accidents can easily happen.

Grand Designs

REDESIGN. The Empire State Building has been designed by architects Shreve and Lamb, who've changed their design for the tower several times.

1928. The first design is for a tower with 50 stories.

14

Your Working Day

START. Be on-site by 3:30 a.m. The beams arrive at dawn each day, and you have to start working as soon as they're unloaded.

Talk about fast food!

FINISH. After a 13-hour day, you finish at 4:30 p.m.

LUNCH. You'll have just 30 minutes to eat your lunch.

Handy Hint

Work fast! With so much steel coming in, there's not a minute to lose.

PAY. For a full day's work, you'll be paid about $26— that's $2 per hour.

1929. The design is then enlarged to 65 stories.

1929. Then it becomes an 80-story tower, almost 1,000 feet (304 m) high.

But across town, the brand-new Chrysler Building is rising to 1,048 feet (319 m).

1929. Not to be outdone, the architects add six stories to the Empire State Building, making it 1,050 feet (320 m) high—the world's tallest tower. (A mast at the top was added later.)

Get Up! Going to Work

The tower rises at an incredible speed—four and a half stories every week! It's been planned so carefully that it's like putting together a jigsaw puzzle, with every beam fitting into its proper place. The higher it rises, the higher you have to go to work. Workers on other skyscrapers get exhausted from climbing steps and ladders. But it's different on the Empire State Building. There are several elevators, some of them saved from the old Waldorf-Astoria Hotel, and you travel to your floor quickly and easily. But be sure you don't fall down an open elevator shaft—it's a long way to the bottom.

Arrghh!!

Danger Zone!

FATAL ACCIDENT. During the building of the steel frame, one man loses his life when he falls down an elevator shaft.

How Many Men?

WORKFORCE. Thousands of men work on the tower. The greatest number working at any one time is 3,439, on Thursday, August 14, 1930.

Electrician

Cook

Water boy

Bricklayer

Plumber

Steel man

Carpenter

16

Catch! Joining the Beams

Watch where you're throwing that thing!

This is a noisy site. Most of the noise comes from the riveters—workers who join steel beams together with rivets. You're a catcher in one of the 40 riveting gangs, and on a good day your team can fix 500 rivets, for which you'll earn $1.92 an hour. You have to concentrate on this job. Not only do you have to catch red-hot rivets flung to you by the furnace man, but you've got to get them to the bucker-up man before they cool and become too hard to shape. The gunman's air gun, or jackhammer, bashes each rivet twice a second to flatten its head. The noise is enough to make you deaf—if you're not already deaf from operating a drill!

Did I tell you about my time as a catcher?

Yes. It was riveting.

How to Rivet a Beam

1. THE FURNACE MAN heats a rivet—a short, strong steel rod—until it's soft enough to be hammered into shape.

2. HE FLICKS the red-hot rivet to the catcher.

3. THE CATCHER catches the rivet in a tin bucket.

4. HE PLACES the rivet in a hole drilled through two beams.

5. THE BUCKER-UP MAN holds the rivet in place.

6. THE GUNMAN hammers the rivet with a jackhammer. This flattens the head of the rivet, so it can't fall out of its hole.

Handy Hint

Ouch!

Don't get burned! The rivets are red-hot, so remember to wear thick gloves.

Danger Zone!

FATAL ACCIDENT. A swinging hoist hits a man and kills him.

ON SEPTEMBER 15, 1930, the steelwork is finished on the top floor. The flag is raised in a ceremony known as "topping out."

Sky Boy! A Good Head for Heights

As the tower rises, crowds gaze up from the streets far below. They watch in amazement as you walk along the narrow beams and climb up and down steel cables. Is it any wonder they call you a "sky boy"? Of all the skywalkers working on the Empire State Building, the bravest are the Mohawk ironworkers—Native Americans with nerves of steel and seemingly no fear of heights. They make the work look easy, but it's very dangerous. One little slip is all it would take to send you plunging to the street. But no sky boy has ever fallen off the tower. Let's keep it that way, OK?

He'd better start flapping.

Yikes! That was my best cap!

20

For the Record

SMILE, PLEASE. A famous photographer has been hired to photograph the workers as they go about their jobs. If Mr. Lewis Hine points his camera at you, keep still while he takes your photograph.

Handy Hint

When you're on a beam, don't look down. Just look to the end of the beam and keep walking. That way you'll keep your balance.

Food and Drink

THIRSTY WORK. You can have as much water as you like—just ask a water boy to bring some to you. But don't stop working!

LUNCH TIME. Listen for the whistle at noon—your 30-minute lunch break starts now.

Fweeet!!

EAT OUT. If you don't want a hot meal, buy sandwiches and coffee and enjoy the view.

What's in yours?

EAT IN. For 40 cents, you can have a hot meal and a slice of pie in an on-site cafe.

21

The Hard Stuff!

As soon as the steel for a new story is in place, teams of workers start on the floors, walls, and windows. After your scary work as a sky boy, you thought anything would be safer—but think again. As a bricklayer, you've got to lay bricks for the tower's outer walls. Each story needs about 100,000 bricks, and they've got to be laid in a day. You work on the outside of the building, on a wooden platform called a scaffold. There's danger all around—from falling objects and weak handrails to loose bricks.

Building Materials

STONE. The outside of the building is covered with a skin of smooth limestone, brought from a quarry in Indiana, about 800 miles (1,287 km) away.

WINDOWS. The tower has 6,400 windows. All the window frames are painted a deep red color on the outside.

BRICKS. Ten million bricks are used to build the walls. Trucks tip tons of new bricks into hoppers, and the bricks slide down into dump cars. The cars are hoisted up to the bricklayers.

Danger Zone!
FATAL ACCIDENT. A worker has fallen off the scaffold and plunged to his death.

Weather Warning!

AS IF YOU DIDN'T have enough to worry about—nature can also cause problems.

World's Tallest Tower!

WIND. It's far too dangerous to walk on the steel beams in windy weather.

On December 11, 1929, you hear some breaking news. The entire workforce is talking about the tower's new height. Instead of stopping at 1,050 feet (320 m), the skyscraper's final height will be 1,250 feet (381 m). The final 200 feet (61 m) will be a mast to which airships can be tethered. Airships are the aircraft of the future, and passengers will be able to fly to and from the very heart of New York City. It'll take just seven minutes to travel by elevator from street level to an airship. Meanwhile, you must steady your nerves as the last steel beams for the airship mast are placed.

COLD. In cold weather, your fingers get stiff and numb. It's difficult to hold on to tools and equipment.

RAIN. In wet weather, the steel beams are slippery. Take extra care when you're walking on them.

Airship mooring mast

*I wonder how long it would take to hit the ground from here? *

Handy Hint

Plan ahead for whatever the weather will be. Check the weather report in the newspaper every day.

Airship

GOLDEN RIVET. To mark the placing of the final beam, Al Smith, president of the construction company, drives the last rivet home. It's made of solid gold!

*I marvel at these steelworkers. *

* A person falling from 1,250 feet (381 m) would reach the ground in about nine or ten seconds.

* Al Smith's actual words.

25

Sparks Fly!

The walls, floors, and windows are in place. Now it's time to turn the tower into an office building. Carpenters, plasterers, plumbers, and electricians arrive to build the interior of the skyscraper. There's an increased fire risk from all the flammable materials they are using. Watchmen tour the building regularly, checking for signs of fire. Be careful around those miles of electrical cables—you wouldn't want to go down in history as the person who set fire to the Empire State Building!

Fire!

NOVEMBER 1930. At about 6:00 a.m., a small fire breaks out in a lunch room on the 47th floor. The fire department soon puts it out.

Finishing Materials

PLASTER. Bare walls are covered with a smooth layer of plaster.

WOOD. Carpenters fit doors, panels, and baseboards in place.

MARBLE. Colored marble from France, Germany, Belgium, and Italy decorates the entrance lobby.

Danger Zone!

FATAL ACCIDENT.
A carpenter has lost his life. He was hit by one of the small trucks used to move materials around the site.

Job Done!

You've risked your life on the world's tallest building, and after one year and 45 days, the job is done. The tower was supposed to be finished by May 1931, but you, and thousands of others, have worked long hours and finished the skyscraper in April—a whole month ahead of schedule. The building will open for business on May 1. You can hold your head high, knowing that your hard work has paid off.

How Bad Is Bad?

NO WORK. As the Great Depression bites deeper, it's even harder to find work. In 1931, there are 50 percent fewer building jobs in New York City than in 1930.

EMPIRE STATE

Did I really build that?

What Now?

But what's next? Once again, you're out of work. Building jobs in the city are scarcer than ever, and as unemployment rises, there are more people looking for work. After a few years, you have no choice but to accept handouts from the government. Without them, you'd starve. Even the Empire State Building itself is in trouble. By opening day, only 23 percent of the offices have been rented out, and plans to tie airships to the mast have been abandoned. And the Great Depression isn't over yet.

*EMPIRE STATE
BUILDING
AT A GLANCE*

*Start: March 1930
Finish: April 1931
Build time: 410 days
Height: 1,250 feet
(381 m)
Cost: $24,718,000
Floors: 103
Steps: 1,860
Windows: 6,400
Workers: About 3,400
Weight: About 365,000
tons
Fatalities: 6
Time capsule: Hidden in
the cornerstone*

*The Empire State
Building remained the
world's tallest building
until 1972.*

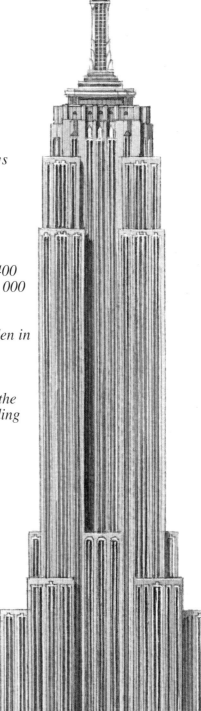

ACROSS AMERICA, about one sixth of all American workers are out of work — around 8 million people in total.

BREAD LINE. When your unemployment money runs out, stand in line to wait for your daily handout of food.

RELIEF LINE. You'll have to live off unemployment relief — money from the government.

Glossary

Air gun A hammer powered by compressed air; also called a jackhammer.

Airship A type of aircraft filled with a lighter-than-air gas. It looks like a giant, thin balloon.

Bedrock The solid rock that lies underneath loose soil.

Black Tuesday October 29, 1929. On this day the stock market crashed in the United States, costing many companies millions of dollars.

Blaster A person who works with explosives.

Bread line A line of unemployed people waiting to be given free food.

Bucker-up man In a riveting gang, the man who held the rivet steady with an iron bar while it was hammered by the gunman.

Catcher In a riveting gang, the man who caught a rivet thrown to him by the furnace man.

Concrete A mixture of cement, sand, and gravel that sets into a strong, solid material.

Debris Loose rock or rubble.

Derrick A crane with a long reach.

Dynamite A type of explosive.

Flammable Liable to catch fire.

Furnace man In a riveting gang, the man who heated a rivet until it was red-hot, making it soft enough to hammer into shape.

Great Depression A time in the late 1920s and much of the 1930s when many people in America, and other countries, were out of work.

Ground man One of the men who worked in a steam shovel team. He guided the bucket or shovel to the right place on the ground.

Gunman In a riveting gang, the man who used an air gun, or jackhammer, to flatten the head of a rivet in order to join two pieces of steel together.

Hopper A funnel-shaped container.

Jackhammer A hammer powered by compressed air; also called an air gun.

Marble A type of stone that can be polished to make long-lasting walls and floors.

Relief line A line of unemployed people waiting to be given unemployment money, which was paid to them by the government.

Rivet A short metal rod used to attach one piece of metal to another. The end of the rivet was hammered until it flattened out. This prevented it from falling out of its hole.

Scaffold A temporary walkway made from planks of wood.

Sky boy A nickname for a man who worked at great heights during the building of a skyscraper.

Skyscraper A very tall building.

Steam crane A machine powered by steam that raises and lowers heavy objects.

Steam shovel A machine powered by steam that digs or shovels loose ground.

Story One floor of a building.

Tongs A tool used to hold something that is dangerous to hold in the hand, such as a hot rivet.

Topping out A ceremony held by builders to mark the completion of the highest point of a new building.

Watchman A workman who watches out for problems, especially fires.

Water boy A young man who carried drinking water to the workmen, and sprinkled water onto the floors to settle the dust.

Wrecker A person whose job is to demolish (pull down) a building.

Index